Fading

Into

the

Clouds

Also by Deonte' Earl Towner

(POETRY)

Pieces in the Dark: Turn the Light On
Secretly Unhappy: Please Don't Tell

Fading

Into

the

Clouds

Deonte' Earl Towner

Printed in the United States of America

First Printing, 2021

Instagram: deontetowner
Cover Design: Alejandro Baigorri
ISBN: 978-0-578-82234-1

To those who keep finding and losing themselves.

Open letter
2:12 AM Cold Winter Apartment

Is anyone truly living their best life or is it a performance that we put on for our followers on social media? We have created a world of illusions when in reality we are far from who we pretend to be online. As we scroll there are couples that show us how exciting and happy their relationship is, but in reality, the lovebirds have been arguing for more than half of their relationship. One is sleeping in the main room and the other is sleeping on the couch. The communication is lacking and the distance is becoming more apparent. We are too embarrassed to walk away and change our status to single because of the fear of online judgment.

As we sit home wishing we had a big circle of friends we come across a post of people posing for a picture at a party. In reality, the friendships in the group is made up of betrayal, hidden jealousy, secret affairs and suppressed past hurts that have never been resolved.
As we continue to scroll we see our favorite social media influencers. We love to see how glamorous their life is, the amount of endless cash they flaunt, the big house, lavish weekend adventures, expensive bags and designer clothes we can't afford. In reality, they

are spiritually empty on the inside, tossing and turning every night because of how much they have changed themselves to be someone they are not to keep their followers on social media. They have become exhausted with all of the content they are making for the world.

There are days we all hate social media. We want to log out or simply delete it but we know that in order to stay connected to the world then we must stay on. The first thing we do in the morning and at night is check our phone. We promise ourselves before we fall asleep that this is the last scroll. We find ourselves scrolling a few more hours and then look on the far-left corner of our phone while it reads 2AM.

I wonder what will be our last post on social media before we leave to the afterlife. Will it be a sad message? Will it be a funny post or maybe our favorite corrido song as we are out with friends singing at the top of our lungs thinking about all of our toxic exes? Will we even be logged on? Or, will it land on a day we are taking a social media break logged off from the rest of the world? However, our life may end I hope we find joy, happiness, satisfaction, inner peace and not leave this earth scrolling wishing that we had someone else's life that we saw on social media.

Quarantine Blues

Sometimes it is a struggle to get out of bed.
I try my hardest to be positive, but
depression is always lurking around the
corner waiting for a sad thought.

I scroll through social media and I see
vendors getting attacked, people dying from
the virus, people getting killed on the streets,
peaceful protestors crying for change,
mothers pleading for justice, ex-lovers
exposing each other through screenshots,
people arguing on social media over
movements and politics.

It's becoming too much to handle. My
anxiety and depression are starting to
become soulmates. Every time I split the
two they find reasons to be together again.
Still holding on to hope for this bad dream
to be over one day.

Uber Friends

I loved everyone but myself. I made people happy when they were sad, but for years I failed to be there for myself. I was hurting and ignoring my feelings to make sure I could bring joy to others. No matter what time of the day or night it was people could always count on me to answer my phone. I always imagined to have someone do that for me. It seemed as though whenever people were happy they would leave.

Whenever people got clarity for their problem they would leave. When people found love they would leave. When people finally moved on from their ex they would leave. When people had their life figured out they would leave. They always leave but alone is exactly how I should be.

Before You Walk Out

Once you walk out of this room don't come back. Rethink what you are leaving behind.

Don't get yourself stuck in a situation and then come running back because you need someone to comfort you. Let me live my life in peace and allow me to move on. Don't make life harder for me.

Once you walk out those doors don't send me the *I miss you* text whenever you need my warm embrace. My heart doesn't melt for your old tricks anymore. I do not cling to every empty promise that you cry out in desperate attempts to win me over again.

Whoever you left me for lean on them, stay there and don't come back.

Please do it all the time, not sometimes

Words that should melt the average heart are actually thorns and daggers that remind me of the false hope that I used to carry in my youth. The growth and love that I have for myself comes to a halt whenever I fail to hold you accountable because of the countless excuses that I make for your behavior. I try my hardest to not fall so easily so you can see that I am different.

I don't want you to think of me as a discarded object on the floor that you can easily get rid of. I don't want you to think that you can take advantage of my emotions after you have apologized because you know how weak I can be because of my past experiences.

I want you to see that I am not easily impressed, and I can walk away if I need to. I want you to know that I am not one of your past lovers that only falls for the good times. I will not be a part of your rotation schedule. I will not be a part of your generational cycle of abuse.

Hey Stranger

You were upset with yourself all along. You didn't allow yourself to heal from the past. You put everything on me. You were hoping that my love could comfort all that was broken and undone in your life.

My friendship was something that you weren't used to. You knew that I stayed true to my word and that I would be there for you whenever you needed me. I was there for you so much that I forgot to be there for myself. I began to lose who I was trying to help you. You never asked me for anything because you made the friendship about you. We got close because of all the problems that you were facing in life.

I knew everything about you, but you knew nothing about me.

Born Angry

Who made you think it was alright to hurt
someone, apologize and then do the same
thing again?

Who taught you that love is pain?

Who raised you…?

Soul Ties to You

I need more than an apology. I need you to go back in time and reverse everything that made me fall in love with you. I need you to go back in time and walk away from me when you realized that I had feelings for you. I need you to fight off my love and say *I am not equipped to be in a relationship.* I need you to go back in time and warn me that you are going to break my heart, leave me feeling insecure, broken, hopeless and defeated.

Since you aren't emotionally equipped to do any of those things I am tied in bondage dealing with spiritual warfare and its heavy.

The Break Up Story

There are always two different stories when couples go their separate ways.

One mentions to their friend *it was all their fault.*

The other calls their friend and mentions *I tried my best and they didn't appreciate me.*

Each friend will take a side and begin telling them everything that they want to hear. *You don't need them. They never deserved you. You can do so much better.*

Deep down inside the lovers are secretly thinking of each other. One is stuck in the past and the other feels free even though the memories continue to appear.

One day it will all be too late

Don't allow them to convince you to stay.
You keep making every excuse for them in
your head. People will begin to distance
themselves from you because they will grow
tired of hearing your sad stories. Everyone
will take you as a joke.

People will say *you will go back* whenever
you say *this time I am going to leave for
good.* One day you will wake up years later
realizing that you settled for less.

Back in Time

If you could go back in time what would you have done differently?

Would you have avoided your ex and ignored the first encounter that made you get deep into your feelings for them? Would you have fixed that friendship that you still desire to this day? Would you go harder after your dreams? Would you have moved off to another city instead of allowing fear to get in the way? Would you have saved your body for someone else instead of giving it to the person that you thought would be their forever?

No Ways

I hope you know that I do not have any ill feelings towards you. I know how things ended and the feelings that we had. I can only speak for myself but I don't take back any of the memories that we had with each other. I realized that in order to move on I must delete all of the old photos and videos of us together but those times will forever live in my heart.

Maybe you pushed all of those memories out of your heart, but I didn't even though I tried countless times. They were real and moments like those will never be forgotten but cherished.

Painful Pleasures

No matter how good life is I often think about the past. I try my hardest not to get stuck. I often question if I moved on yet, or are they just memories that will never go away. I can't think about them too much because those old feelings will resurface and then I will become distracted.

My mind is always trying to pull me back there again. Could it be possible that I find comfort in my painful past because I am afraid of future happiness?

Before I met you

You were at war with yourself. Why did you walk into my life and disturb my peace? You tricked me into believing that you would bring love and peace into my life. You pretended to be everything that I wanted and needed. I took a risk and it ended up not being worth it.

Give me back the joy and peace I had prior to meeting you. I began to realize that you couldn't give me any of those things because you never had them yourself. This is not what I want or need. I was so focused before I met you, and now I am stuck in time trying to make sense of why you would make me feel like this after you knew how I was done in the past.

Keep Me in Mind

Before you talk badly about me to your friends remember what we had. Remember all the times you told me that you loved me even though you were hurting me countless times and I forgave you.

Don't forget what I meant to you. Remember how I was there for you when all your friends began betraying you. Don't forget all the times you walked away from me and I allowed you to keep coming back. Whenever your family pushed you away I pulled you into mine. When no one else understood you mentally I helped you make sense of your thoughts. Don't allow your anger and hatred to go so far that you forget about everything I was to you.

Not Enough

Be careful of who you allow back into your life because you miss them. Is it possible that sometimes they need to be out of your life for a while in order to realize what they lost?

I don't want to punish you forever by not allowing you back into my life, but I don't want to ruin my emotional progress over you. There is a huge possibility that you might go back to your old ways. I don't want to force myself to move on again. I have decided to ponder on the memories of us. I am trying to catch myself from having feelings when I think of you.

I will always have a soft spot for you in my heart but this time I choose me first.

Drifting Away

When two people fall in love the beginning of the relationship is perfect. The long good morning text are sent right when you wake up, the beautiful FaceTime calls until you fall asleep, the *no you hang up first is* prolonged and the time seems to flow smoothly the closer you get to each other.

And then one day it all stops. You realize they are falling short of how they used to be in the beginning.

The text messages are getting shorter, the *I've been busy* excuses are beginning to happen more often. The truth in who they really are is beginning to show. You are fighting for the love to last but it seems as though the waves are pushing them further away. You try to remind them of how things used to be but every day they are drifting with the waves. All that you used to have with them is becoming a memory.

spirited away

There were times I would call my friends at night and wonder if you moved on yet. I would replay arguments in my head that we had in the past because of how many times I blamed myself. I humbled myself to understand you even though you didn't do the same. I am gathering my strength back, and now I am only concerned about my happiness.

Heavy Hands

I never understood how much pain I could
hold until I met you. My hands are heavy
and the only way I can get rid of the pain is
if I let go of you.

Show Me

In the beginning of the relationship we pretend to be perfect and we hide what bothers us because we do not want to lose them over the small things. We are very careful with our words and actions. The gentleness that we have for the person begins to fade through time because of how comfortable we become.

The honeymoon stage ends and true colors begin to show. *I don't like when you say that to me. It bothers me when you spend more time with your friends than me. You post on social media but you can't respond back to my message?* Our list of needs and wants begin to pile up and expectations from that person begins to increase. They begin to see what makes us sad, upset and insecure. They begin to see another side of us they didn't see in the beginning. The real process of loving the whole person and not just part of who we think they are begins.

Black Bird

If I was a bird I would fly high in the sky above everything. I wish I could randomly poop on everyone's heads that did me wrong. I would wake up every morning, fly without obligations and have no soul ties to anyone. The freedom within my wings and home be wherever I land.

I would never be locked up listening to orders. I would make my own rules and not be pressured by societies rules to belong or conform. My wings will flap to its own beat and cause others that are on the ground to look up and wonder who I was.

I would sit on the roof of cars, trees and bridges looking into the soulless people passing to their next destination.

Untangled Thoughts

Free yourself from the lies they have told you. Free yourself from the insecurities they have tried to burden you with. Free yourself from the nights you cried over them. Free yourself from the thoughts of never finding someone better.

Free yourself from the voices that tell you *everything is your fault*. Free yourself from thinking life would be better without you here. Free yourself from the echoes that tell you that *you are all alone and no one loves you.*

Not Acceptable

I refuse to allow you to walk all over me. I know who I am. I will not allow you to call me out of my name whenever you get mad at me. I am worthy of love and respect. This is not love this is you throwing all your insecurities on me. I am not built to hold all your wrath and trauma.

You can apologize all you want but I am not going to cuddle you and say that it is alright and allow the cycle to repeat itself. Me holding on to you is me betraying who I am and what I stand for.

I will not make excuses for your behavior. I have too much pride and self-worth to endure abuse. I was once wounded in the past. At one point in my life I would have allowed this type of treatment but not anymore.

Private Relationships

I'm tired of everyone tearing us apart. If it's not your friends then it's your family. And if it's not your family it's people on social media. There is no peace in this relationship. I wish you were strong enough to block out the unnecessary voices.

You used to say *it's you and I against the world*. And now it's starting to feel like it's me against everyone. I feel the battle is coming to an end. At the end of the battle I see myself alone without you. I see you realizing years later that I was right from the start and it was only everyone trying to tear us apart.

It will all be too late because I will be moved on with my life either by myself or with someone else. I hope you see before it's too late because you are only forcing me to make decisions I don't want to make.

Holding it down on earth while you're in heaven

I remember when I got the call that you were gone. I thought I had all the time in the world to spend with you. Even though I only knew you for a couple of years it felt like we grew up together. You understood my problems more than anyone. They don't make them like you in the world anymore. Whenever I am having a bad day I begin to think about the times we shared. The times we laughed at things we weren't supposed to make fun of. The times when you saw someone I didn't like and you would say *there goes your best friend*. The times I was worried about my future and you would remind me of who God created me to be and how I am the strongest person you've ever met. So many things I wish I could've said to you before your left. So many memories I wish we could relieve together. So many places I would've loved to travel with you. I want to be mad at you because you left me in a world full of chaos but I understand that I need to hold it down for the both of us on earth. I have to keep your memory alive and tell your story.

Holding Back

Say what's on your heart. Don't be afraid to hurt me. Lay it on the table. There's nothing you can say that I won't heal from.

Speak from the heart even if you don't think I am going to like it.

Let the tears flow.

Let the wrath fall from your lips and may I be strong enough to move on.

Another cold night

While the music played I began tossing and turning thinking about the years that I wasted my life searching for love. The failed relationships and the toxic behavior I allowed in my space.

I realized that the love I was searching for was already inside of me. I thought the source was in another person. I laid everything down for a human being that would never do the same for me. I made sacrifices for someone that would never do the same for me.

As my eyes were beginning to shut I vowed to never neglect myself for love.

After the Break Up

Don't fade away. You are not done. Keep going after your dreams and continue to live. Don't allow anything to burn your heart out. You have something inside of you that others need.

The beautiful soul that God created inside of you is meant to be used for his glory. You were meant to bring joy, love and friendship to others that you come across.

Through the pain you must fight to keep loving others. Allow yourself to feel the sadness that visits you periodically throughout the day because you haven't moved on.

I know you have heard it all before but just know one day everything you are feeling will all end.

First Instincts

As months dragged by I realized that
nothing will ever change.

I could either grow old and miserable with
you, or I could walk away, find freedom
through my strength, and take a chance by
finding love in someone else.

Optional Healing

In order to heal everything has to come out.
Sometimes you have to relive memories that
you don't want to think about anymore.
Healing requires the mask that we put on
social media to come off.

Healing requires people to judge us. Healing
causes us to wake up with glossy eyes in the
morning as we are holding on to hope
praying we make it through the day without
taking all of our feelings out on people that
love us. Healing causes us to look down as
we are brushing our teeth because we are too
ashamed to look at ourselves in the mirror.

Some people will never find healing because
the process is too painful for them to bear. In
life we make choices and if we want to find
peace then healing is the only option that
will give us everlasting joy in our hearts.

Love on the Road

Let's go on a drive and get away from all the cares in the world.

I know that we have been busy and we haven't really made time for each other. Let's take this moment to forget about everything. Let's go back to how things used to be. Let the corridos play as I hold your hand and look at you without words.

Let's not argue or stress about anything. Let's go wherever the road takes us. Just the two of us.

Me, you and the road.

Clarity in the Mind

I completely changed for you. I took up for you. I told my family and friends lies to prove everything they said about you was wrong. I beat myself down to fit the image you wanted me to be. I was always there for you anytime you needed me. It still wasn't good enough for you. You still left me, and now I feel foolish for how much I played myself. I pretend to have so much pride and self-worth but I forfeited my peace for your love and attention.

Maybe this says more about me than you. Maybe I am not as strong as I portray to be. What we had exposed all that I lacked in myself. Instead of being angry at you, I should be grateful that you helped me realize that I don't have it all together.

I take back every bad thing I said about you because I began focusing on you instead of what I needed to work on.

Looking Up

Who were you before the relationship?

Who were you before you started your career? Who were you before you became successful?

Are you happier now or did you lose yourself along the way?

Give It Time

Sometimes speaking from the heart means hurting the one you love. Sometimes it means telling them that the relationship is over and there is nothing else to give. Sometimes it means going back on your promises by no longer being there for them forever. Sometimes speaking from the heart means hurting yourself because of how painful the truth is.

People often say that the truth will set you free, but no one tells you how painful freedom can be in the process. The war in the soul of speaking from the heart, knowing you hurt the one you love can become hard to move on from. Love comes with being honest.

Sometimes love means walking away so you can both be free. It may not feel good in the moment but through time it will all make sense.

All in My Head

Get out of bed. Don't waste another day regretting the past. I know they meant the world to you and the absence of them is making your head spin with questions.

You are probably wondering *how did they move on so fast.* Stop checking your phone and looking at their Instagram page. Delete all of their videos and pictures.

Get rid of everything that reminds you of them, but one thing you will never get rid of is the way you first met.

Nothing Is Wrong

We have become experts at making excuses for why we are single. Our family and friends love to ask

Why are you single?

The rehearsed responses we give are *oh I am focusing on myself. I haven't found the right one yet. I am too busy. I am practicing self-love It's not God's time yet.*

We begin to wonder if there is something wrong with us. *Is it okay to be single at this age? Am I good enough for love?* We begin to feel insecure all over again. And if we aren't confident we will find ourselves staying up all night tossing and turning replaying the questions centered around our non-existent love life.

We may even start scrolling through social media and become bitter because we are still single and it seems as though the rest of the world has found love. We must stay encouraged and not compare who we are based on everyone's expectations of us.

Headaches

When we hug I can feel that you are ready to let go when we embrace. The conversations we have on the phone are becoming shorter every day. The kisses that we share have no passion behind them.

We are going through the motions and it is sending me over the edge. We are losing patience for each other. We find ourselves arguing over little things and not recovering from them.

Every day I wake up with a headache ready to give up. Why are we holding on to something that we both refuse to repair? I can't seem to remember the last encounter we had without pushing each other away. At first you wanted me, and now you don't know what you want. I am becoming someone you choose to deal with instead of someone you love and want to spend forever with.

Texting Me Under the Influence

Can you please answer your phone? I can't stop thinking about you. I am never going to find anyone that is going to put up with me like you do.

My heart feels empty without you. I find myself partying and drinking my sorrows away. If only you were here I could show you how much I changed. If you love me then you would give me another chance.

I know that I said hurtful things and kept pushing you away but this time it will be perfect between us. I won't take my anger out on you. I won't put my friends before you.

Please just give me one more chance.

My Ex

Depression secretly whispers *happiness will never come* even though everything is going right. You constantly have to fight against yourself.

Every day you experience random battles and when night time falls that's when the biggest war begins. It can be hard to explain to someone that doesn't deal with the same battles.

Depression will tell you *keep everything to yourself because no one will understand.* Depression is like an ex that won't leave even though you tried everything to get rid of them.

Hidden Secrets

There is a war stirring inside of our souls.
We often do things that aren't spiritually
healthy for us. Sometimes we want to stop
and give up these pleasures but they have
held us for so long we do not know how we
would be without them. The secrets we keep
from others and the lies we tell ourselves
only cause us to be in denial.

Just this last time.

The last time becomes each day and then
years begin to pass. We become disgusted
and angry with ourselves. We go days,
weeks, months and even sometimes a year
but then we go back. Every time we fail we
feel defeated and not good enough.

Friendly Reminder

There are some people that need to stay in your past no matter how much they change. You must not give them an opportunity to hurt you like they did when you put your complete trust in them.

Don't forget how far you've come. Don't forget how much they made you cry in the past. Don't forget how much they lied, told you they will change and never did. Don't forget how hopeless and weak they made you feel when they didn't stick to their commitment.

Don't forget how much power you hold within and how much more you will receive from someone that is willing to give you the amount of love, joy and peace that you would offer them.

Sore Eyes

No matter how much you change people will try to define you from the past. They will bring up the heartache you caused a friend that was close to them. People will remind you of past embarrassing mistakes that you regret every day. Sometimes people will believe rumors that people have spread about you.

As I mature over time I begin to realize that no matter what people say I am only in charge of my feelings and reactions. When you know who you are nothing can stop you from walking in your purpose. You are a villain in someone's eyes, and no matter how much you change people will hold you to your past. You can either stay in the past, cry about it or move on.

No longer myself

If you let a person beat you down long enough you will begin to forget how powerful you are. Every ounce of confidence you have on the inside will be taken away by their harsh words mixed in with their *I love you.*

Their sweet words will overtake you but then when they see you get too confident they will tear you down and tell you to humble yourself. One day you will wake up and realize that you don't have to put up with how they are making you feel.

Alone at the Beach

Last night I dreamt about us at the beach. I had my head on your lap while you were scrolling through your phone laughing at memes. Everything seemed so peaceful and calm. You would randomly tickle me as I was trying to rest, and then I would playfully take your phone away.

All of a sudden a grey cloud rolled in and the waves began to get closer. I began to feel alone. I was no longer safe anymore. The fog began to roll in and garbage began to appear on the beach.

I turned around and you were gone.

Talking to Myself

What do you want from me? How much more do I have to take? Why are you punishing me? I am not your past and I cannot heal you from everyone that hurt you. I don't deserve this but I know it is worth it. What if you never see me for who I am?

I don't want to waste my years on you when I can be with someone that will appreciate the love and effort that I am putting into the relationship. One day I am going to wake up and realize that the grass is greener on the other side. Sometimes happiness means leaving the one you're with in order to find what you have been searching for. Truth be told I need to stop living based off emotions. You have been hurt countless times to the point that you will never see my pure motives. I must pack up and leave.

Maybe I am doing you a favor by leaving. Maybe you will use this time to heal. Or maybe you will get into a relationship and abuse someone else because of your past.

Gasping for Air

I have taken the time to heal. The pain that I was feeling wasn't towards you but it was towards myself. I know that you caused a lot of it, but I can no longer blame you. I allowed myself to ignore all the warning signs. Instead I want to say *thank you for everything.*

I am worth more than you had to offer. I am releasing you from my past, present and future. I am pretty sure there will be days that I will still mourn over you not because I miss you but because of how much it hurt at the time. How I am feeling is very complex. The demons I fight in my mind, mixed with life being hard and then us separating made it more challenging. I am getting better and the light at the end of the tunnel is beginning to appear. I am fighting to reassure myself that I will make it. Every time someone ask me how I am doing I reply with *hanging on in there.*

Left Behind

I wanted you to run after me. I wanted you
to tell me not to let you go. I wanted you to
plead for me to stay. I wanted you to lie and
tell me that you will change. I wanted you to
keep choosing me even if that meant it was
out of empty promises. I wanted to be
caught between your lies, and the scattered
good times we had with each other.

You loved me enough to give me what I
needed and that involved letting go even if it
hurt me.

Done for Good

There are some conversations you have to be done with. There are some memories you can't go back to. There are some stories you can't keep telling others. There are some people you can't let back in. Even when you are tempted to go back you have to constantly remind yourself to move forward.

Don't allow the past to rob your future. Stop allowing things that happened years ago drag you back to that place in your mind. Choose happiness every day you wake up.

Even if you do not feel it in your soul continue to coach yourself that you deserve to feel peace in your mind. Even if what happened in the past was your fault it is time to move forward.

Endless Rounds of Love

Fight the insecurities that keep rising in your mind during the relationship. Breathe and don't allow your past to ruin a good thing. Allow them to fully love you. Don't question their faithfulness. Accept them for being the love of your life and don't fight their gentleness.

This is how love is supposed to feel. It can be scary when all you are used to is being hurt. Tear down those walls. Even if they end up like everyone else I promise that you will get through this. I know you are tired of getting through everything, but you can't allow anything to stop you from loving.

Sometimes people find true love on their first round, sometimes it takes years and multiple partners to find true love. The day will come when you don't have to search anymore and you will then realize that it was all worth it.

Feel my Pain

Stop telling people *it's alright* whenever they hurt your feelings. Don't allow anyone to cry themselves out of a situation because they feel bad for hurting you. Let them sit in their sadness and deal with their feelings by themselves. Don't comfort them. Take your hand off of their shoulder. Stop wiping their tears away with the tissues in your hands.

Remind yourself of how low you felt when they hurt you. Remind yourself of how worthless and isolated you felt when they treated you without a care in the world. Be strong and allow people to deal with the war in their soul on their own.

I know that it doesn't feel good to watch them suffer, but in order for them to stay in your life then they have to change their ways.

Therapist or Friend?

Am I just a resting point for you to stop by whenever things aren't going right in your life? Do you think it's my job to keep picking you up when life gets hard for you? What part do you play in my life? Are you there for me whenever I feel like giving up?

No, because you leave me by myself to deal with everything alone.

Only Human

Do not look at me as a King or a Queen. I am not a superhuman. I do not possess super powers. I have feelings. I have limitations and cannot do everything. I am not an angel, and I am not here to save you. Look at me beyond my skin color.

Look at me beyond my accomplishments, opinions and politics. Look at me beyond my post. I fall at times and make mistakes. Sometimes I go against what I preach. I have mood swings and say things I shouldn't. Let me be a human being and respect me for where I am at.

On My Own

I reached out for my phone to text you, but then I realized I have to be strong and resist the urge to contact you. I have to face this on my own. You are no longer in my life, and I have to find the strength to get through it without you.

I don't want to be predictable. I don't want you to think that I am weak or that I need you. I want you to think that I completely moved on. I want you to think that I am happy even though I am struggling to navigate through life without you.

We were on a journey together, but somewhere along the way you dropped out. Maybe you did me a favor by leaving so I could realize how strong I am alone.

Religious Mirror

Stop telling yourself that you are not good enough. Stop beating yourself up over past mistakes you cannot control. Stop comparing your life to everyone else on social media. You are brave. You are beautiful on the inside out. There is no one like you. You are more than a stupid rate or to be honest game on social media.

Stop worrying about how others perceive you. Whenever you feel sad on the inside think about how much love you have to offer the world. Don't allow anyone to take that away from you. Sometimes you look too much at what others are doing. You have more than others will ever have. You have been through countless trials and tribulations when in actuality if others experienced what you been through they wouldn't of made it. You are special and rare.

Stop forgetting who you are.

It's Me or Them

Don't fight to be in anyone's life.

If someone doesn't see the light in you then let them go. It becomes hard when it's someone you've invested into and then all of a sudden they change.

They begin to listen to their friends more than you. They end up believing the opinions of outsiders. The questions they are beginning to ask you are rumors stemmed from the past. Every day they are beginning to choose everyone but you.

Normal

It's okay to be sad. It's okay to not be good all the time. It's okay to have mood swings and scream at the top of your lungs. It's okay to have arguments with people in your mind. It's okay to cry and then laugh 10 seconds later. It's okay to ignore everyone.

It's okay to say *no!*

It's okay to go low instead of taking the high road at times. It's okay to not be perfect all the time. It's okay to hold on to past hurts and slowly let it go. It's okay that you still think about your ex from time to time even though you are in a new relationship. It's okay to be misunderstood. It's okay that you don't fit in the crowd. It's okay that you look and dress differently than everyone else.

It's okay...

Hurtful Thoughts

The thought of you comes and goes. I often think about how you are feeling when you are deep inside of your covers. I thought we could get through anything. I convinced myself that we were better than that. I thought our love was beyond love. As I let go you never fought back to be in my life.

Did you know that it was over before I did?

Maybe you prepared yourself for the end before I realized it was done. Even though you were still in my life the feelings began to drift away. Time proved that we would be better off without each other. I remember when I used to be important to you, and now I am spending my days being important to myself.

Every day I am building myself up with positive words because I am tired of breaking down. This time I am going to stand.

Endless Times

I hold on to how things used to be. It pains me that those good times are over. People always tell me that there are many more beautiful days ahead. Life goes by so fast and I wish it would slow down at times.

Friendships are fading away. Everyone is going their separate ways. Family members are passing away and people are beginning to outgrow each other. The memories are mixed with sadness and grief.

I wonder if I am the only one that thinks about how everything used to be? Am I stuck in time refusing to let go? I have moved on with my life but my thoughts haven't.

Closed for the Night

I want to be open with you. I want to tell you that your actions and words offend me. I want to tell you my life story, but I know that you are too closed minded.

You will invalidate my feelings and tell me that I am *trippin, too soft* and that I need to *get over it.*

I need to get away from you, but I am not willing to give up the good moments that we shared with each other. It's hard thinking about having to start over with someone else, but I know that I will be happier.

Maybe I don't care about being happy anymore since I have become used to the way you treat me. Or maybe the disrespect that you have been showing me is a form of you trying to hint that you have given up on me and that I need to accept the truth.

Shifting Winds

Stop overthinking they say.

How can I?

It's easier to prepare for bad situations because that's all I know.

Is the universe punishing me?

Choose Wisely

You will find someone else. The last relationship only grew you, and it doesn't define you. It doesn't hold the power to stop you from entering healthy relationships.

You can end the cycle of toxic partners once you recognize what you deserve and what you don't want. You don't have to settle.

Nobody is perfect but there are some things you don't have to put up with.

To Myself

Don't be afraid to be alone. There is nothing wrong with spending your nights listening to music, watching television, video chatting a friend, going places alone or thinking about the future in your head. The insecurities we sometimes feel when we see others on social media out with the crowd can cause us to sometimes compare ourselves to the person we see on the screen.

You are where you are supposed to be. Rest your body and mind. You had a long week. You deserve to stay in. You don't have to go out and entertain everyone with a fake smile pretending to have fun for social media.

Ease your mind and don't allow the outside world to shake you up. There is nothing wrong with you. Don't look for your value by the standards and actions of others on a screen.

Pulling the Plug

The relationship was coming to an end. It became a game. Who is going to pull the plug? As we looked into each other's eyes knowing that our time was running out. We still stayed trying our hardest to enjoy our last few months with each other. No one wanted to address the elephant in the room.

We were both too weak to let go of a future we thought would last forever. Will the relationship end this week? Will it end this month? We were slowly accepting the fact that things were ending and we were both changing. Will this be a cliché break up? Would we use the classic movie line? *It's not you, it's me.*

Will we listen to our sad corridos playlist, with our favorite oversized black depressed looking hoodie, pacing back and forth in our room writing subliminal post on social media trying to convince ourselves that we don't need each other? However, it won't be easy when it ends.

Someone Out There

Imagine being with someone that calls the shots, tells you what time dinner will be and surprises you with plans for the weekend. After a long day of work someone to hold.

Someone that helps you let go of your fears. Someone that sees you struggling with groceries and begins to help you carry them. Someone that will tell you to put down your phone and go to sleep because you have an early start in the morning. Someone that says you are eating too many sweets and it isn't good for your teeth. Someone that sees you starring at your body in the mirror, creeps up behind and says *you are perfect just for me.*

Calm Down

Rest your mind.

Walk away.

You don't have to react. Everything doesn't deserve a response or explanation. You have the right to say no and move on. You choose what you want to invest your energy and thoughts into. Don't allow yourself to lose control. Don't give your power to anyone. Make decisions without asking others what you should do. You are in control of your life.

You are in the driver's seat. If you make the wrong decision get back up and try something new. Don't stay down.

Time to Myself

I need a day to give back to myself.

A day where I don't worry about anything that has been bothering me.

A day with no tears, depression or anxiety. I need a day where I can distance myself from everyone.

A day where my thoughts don't attack me. A day my body can feel the love I am giving it.

A day where I heal, lay everything down at the alter and not pick it back up.

For those who cannot come out

Don't allow them to make you feel guilty for walking away. They kept hurting you. They did everything to prove to you that they were never going to change. You're going to develop into a better person without them.

Hold your head up high for choosing yourself after all these years. Think about all the people in the world who are suffering right now in a toxic relationship. You broke the cycle and now you are able to help so many others through your story.

You're going to be a symbol of hope to the wounded souls who cannot come out by themselves. Now go and take care of yourself... heal.

Acknowledgments I first give honor to Jesus Christ who is the head of my life. He has been by my side every step of the way. When I was on the verge of taking my own life he stopped me before it was too late.

I thank God for my beautiful parents Joseph and Emily Towner. The only reason why I am living out my dreams today is because they have made tremendous sacrifices. My parents are my best friends. I talk to them on the phone three to four times a day. We have an unbreakable bond.

Also, I thank God for my wonderful siblings Natachiana and Joseph. They have always shared their wisdom in order to direct me in the right path. They have been true examples of positive influences.

To my soon to be sister-in-law Amanda welcome into the family. I love you dearly. When you and Jojo called me with the news of engagement I couldn't stop smiling. You are an angel sent for my brother.

To my brother-in-law Rynell AKA Showbiz you bring laughter to my heart!

To my handsome nephews Rynell Jr and Shelton. I love you as if you were my own kids. I love hearing you all scream *Uncle Dee* as you both open the door to greet me. One day you will be old enough to read this book, but until then enjoy your youth.

To the rock of the family my grandmother we call Big Momma. You remind me that no matter how old I get I am still your big ol baby. Thank you for making me feel like a kid no matter how old I get.

To my beautiful readers I call my friends and family on social media, Salinas, the 831, my students and everyone around the world. You all remind me every day that I am not alone. Some of you struggle each day but yet still get up every morning because of the small amount of hope you are holding on to. You all have supported me throughout all my goals and new adventures. I thank you for the words of encouragement on social media. I haven't met a lot of you in person but we talk everyday as though we have known each other for years. I thank you for the closeness that we share.

Thanks for being open to sharing your stories with me on social media. We have had days where we all prayed with each other, laughed and discussed serious topics. Everything you all have told me I will forever hold them in my heart. Let's continue to lift each other up in prayer. We are strong, we are warriors and you all are my friends and family.

Made in the USA
Monee, IL
03 January 2021

56316470R00083